Covenant Bible
Study Series

Presence and Power

by
Robert Dell

faithQuest
Elgin, Illinois

Covenant Bible Study Series
Presence and Power

Copyright © 1991 by Brethren Press

faithQuest, a division of Brethren Press, 1451 Dundee Avenue, Elgin, IL 60120

Biblical quotations, unless otherwise noted, are from the Revised Standard Version of the Bible, copyrighted 1946, 1952, and 1971 by the Division of Christian Education, National Council of Churches, and are used by permission.

Cover design by Jeane Healy

Library of Congress Cataloguing-in-Publication Data

Dell, Robert W.
    Presence and Power / Robert Dell; foreword by
    June Adams Gibble.
          p.   cm. — (Covenant Bible study series)
    ISBN 0-87178-720-2
    1. Bible. N.T. Acts—Study.   I. Title   II. Series
    BS2626.D37   1991
    226.6'06—dc20   90-22124
                                               CIP

Manufactured in the United States of America

Contents

Foreword

My first Bible was a gift from my Landes grandparents on my eighth birthday. With the Bible was a chart to help me read through the Bible, one chapter a day. Full of enthusiasm, I began with Genesis 1, reading day by day through 50 chapters of Genesis and 40 chapters of Exodus. Then came Leviticus and what a change in my enthusiasm for "a chapter a day!" Quickly, I decided that this reading discipline didn't mean I had to go straight through the Bible. I turned to the New Testament and happily read through Matthew, Mark, Luke, and John.

At eight years of age, the power of the biblical story had caught me. The gentle encouragement of grandparents helped to draw me into the faith story of the people of God. The presence and the power of God's Spirit which moved through the story of a long-ago people **was** beginning to touch my life also.

The particular story of God's presence and power in the life of a young church impacted me strongly during my early teen years. I remember a time when I began reading the book of Acts, and how surprised I was that it read "like a real story." No more one-chapter-a-day! This time I read through the whole book, caught up in the sweep of an exciting story. And to this day the message of Acts has had a powerful hold over me, as I sense the Holy Spirit moving among a people, both two thousand years ago and today.

This Bible study, "The Presence and the Power," will draw you into the exciting story of a young church, formed and empowered by the Holy Spirit, struggling and growing as a community of believers, being sent out into the world to witness and to serve. It will challenge you to look at your own lives and the life of your congregation: How are you empowered for new life and mission in today's world?

This relational Bible study is designed for small group settings within the congregation. As you begin your study, you will want to keep in mind some ways in which relational Bible study differs from other kinds of Bible study.

Recognize first that relational Bible study has strong biblical foundations. Anchored in the covenantal history of God and the people, relational Bible study recognizes that God's empowerment comes to the community today as persons gather to pray and to study, to share and to receive, to reflect and to act. Covenant community is necessary for growing up in faith. Such growth does not just happen—it must be struggled for in the power of the Holy Spirit and in accord with the teachings of Jesus.

Relational Bible study takes seriously the corporateness of the faith. The Body of Christ becomes a reality within the life of the group, as each person contributes to the group's study, prayer, and work together. Each one's contribution is needed as the group seeks the meaning of the text. "For just as the body is one and has many members, and all the members of the body, though many, are one body, so it is with Christ. . . . Now you are the body of Christ and individually members of it" (1 Cor. 12:12, 17).

Relational Bible study helps both persons and the group to claim the working of the Holy Spirit in their midst. This kind of small group study knows that ". . . where two or three have met together in my name, I am there among them" (Matt. 18:20).

With these understandings of relational Bible study, you will want to give careful attention to these guidelines:

1. As a small group of learners, we gather around God's Word to discern God's word for us today.
2. The words, stories, and admonitions we find in scripture come alive for us today.
3. All persons are learners and all are leaders; we all come needing to learn, and we all come to "lead," to teach.
4. Each person will contribute to the study, sharing the meaning found in the scripture and helping to bring meaning to others.
5. Trust and vulnerability are needed; we are vulnerable as we share out of our own experience, and in such sharing, we learn to trust others and to be trustworthy.

Welcome to this study of "The Presence and the Power." May you be caught up in this story of the young church, and challenged by the Spirit's work with these first Christians. May you share deeply with sisters and brothers in faith and discover anew God's word for today. And may the Holy Spirit move among you, so that you know "the presence and the power" directing your life.

June Adams Gibble
Elgin, Illinois

1

The Presence And Power Of The Holy Spirit
Acts 2

Preparation

1. Read over Luke quickly to get its major themes in mind. Focus particularly on what is said about the situation of the "post-Resurrection" church.
2. Then read Acts 1—2 more carefully. Write down significant points along with your questions.

Understanding

In Luke, the companion volume to Acts, the risen Christ had declared the disciples "witnesses" of all that had been said and done (Luke 24:44ff.). But they were to wait in Jerusalem until they were "clothed with power from on high." They would need it. What they had to say ran counter to what the world expected.

Most ordinary Jews hoped for a messiah who would restore Israel to a position of dominance in the world. This messiah would bring the wealth of the nations to Jerusalem, rebuild the Temple as God's very footstool on earth, and in particular stomp the Romans into grape juice.

The earliest disciples began their journey with Jesus as "ordinary Jews." Peter, even when he came to believe that Jesus was the Messiah, was unable to comprehend that Jesus would take the role of the "suffering servant" (cf. Mark 8:27–33). Peter's problem was no doubt multiplied in the early church. Even after meeting the resurrected Lord, the disciples asked: "Lord, will you at this time restore the kingdom to Israel?" (Acts 1:6). They still expected a kind of political power to be given them. What they were to receive, however, was not military, political, or economic might, but a new Spirit (Acts 1:8).

To understand what is happening in Acts 2, compare it with John 20:19–23. In John's gospel, Christ gives the Holy Spirit, his Spirit, to the disciples in their first meeting with him as risen Lord. Christ gives the Spirit in order to carry on in the world the very same mission which God had given Jesus. That mission also forms the key to understanding Acts.

The disciples lacked not simply the power to *tell* the story but the power *to be the story*, to carry on the very same mission, to be Christ for their generation. Only by that infusion of Christ's Spirit could they become the very Body of Christ in the world.

As they waited in Jerusalem, they were *all together* (Acts 2:1). We are often tempted to write the importance of the individual just as large in the New Testament as we write it in our culture. Everything, we think, depends upon the individual. Everything is "my" choice. We even assume that the church is a collection of individuals, joined only by their common but individually chosen allegiance to their Lord.

The Apostle Paul wrote to the Corinthians: "Now you are the Body of Christ and individually members of it" (1 Cor. 12:27). Clearly, this reverses our usual notion. It is not the individual, but the church as the *Body* which is prior. From having been "membered into" the Body of Christ we gain our individuality.

This perspective is necessary in order for us to understand how the church, receiving the fire and wind of the Spirit, became the Body of Christ, able to do the work of Christ in the world. The disciples were "all together" and received the Spirit *as the church.*

What, or better, *who* is the Holy Spirit?

The Holy Spirit is the essence of the Eternal God, the same Spirit who dwelt in Jesus and is now given to indwell those who believe in him. We are at the center of the truth when we say that the Holy Spirit was and is the resurrected, ascended, reigning Christ, now among and within his committed followers. (Lloyd Ogilvie, *Drumbeat of Love.*)

That's the key. The Pentecost experience for the church is a *resurrection*! It's a birth! Through this event the church becomes more than a human association. It becomes God's own child, the very body of Christ! Just as God was "in Christ," so Christ is "in the church."

The Spirit gives the church the power to communicate with heart-touching voice and life. Too often we get hung up on the nature and meaning of the "glossolalia," or speaking in tongues. Reflect upon the affirmation in John: "In the beginning was the Word" (John 1:1). Then, says John, that Word became flesh in the birth of Christ in human form. In that form we were able to view what would otherwise be hidden to us—divine glory! The point: we are able to see God's own self-expression in Jesus. Jesus was a "divine utterance"!

Why then would not the church, when it is inspired with the very life of Christ through the coming of the Holy Spirit, also be able to communicate the divine glory? We would expect to be able to say, "In the church, we behold the very glory of God's self-expression." The church becomes the Word of God in the flesh.

In Jerusalem they began "to speak in tongues" (Acts 2:4). Remember Paul's counsel in 1 Corinthians 12–14. Clearly, he felt prophecy was the more helpful utterance. To outsiders the "unintelligible sounds" of tongues-speaking is evidence that the church is full of mad people. But prophecy or preaching will create a clear sense that God is truly present in the church (1 Cor. 14:20ff.). Each ought, Paul admonishes, to desire to communicate intelligibly to outsiders. Each should seek to speak the languages of earth more than of angels (1 Cor. 13:1).

That kind of understanding is also present here in Acts 2. Since some began to speak excitedly in tongues in the manner to which Paul was referring in 1 Corinthians, hearers in Jerusalem did indeed think the Christians were mad, or at least drunk. More appropriate impact came through the "utterances" which could be understood. Persons from all over the known world began to hear the praises of God in their mother tongues, and they listened as they never had before. By far the greatest impact came when the Spirit gave Peter "utterance." The effect of Peter's address upon the hearers was exactly what Paul described in 1 Corinthians. They were "cut to the heart." Some three thousand souls, the scripture says, were added to the kingdom that day.

This tremendous outburst of intelligible, heart-rending communication drawing people of diverse origin into common understanding suggests that the breach of Babel was being healed on the Day of Pentecost (Gen. 11:1–11). Thus is implied the joining of humankind into one family of God. What Paul calls the "dividing wall of hostility" began to be torn down in the miracle of Pentecost.

I suspect that this new community in Christ was in fact the most powerful "utterance" of the Spirit. If we may return to Paul's discussion of tongues and prophecy for a moment, we note that Paul argued persuasively that it was love more than anything else which gave authenticity to the witness of the church (1 Cor. 13). And there is the word of Christ in John 13:34–5 that the disciples' love for one another would proclaim their status as followers of Christ. Little wonder, then, that the giving of the Spirit to the disciples, who were "all together" in anticipation of the "promise of the Father," produced a group which continued to be together in one fellowship concerned with the apostles' teaching, fellowship, eating together, prayer, and mutual concern for one another. It may well have been the expression ("utterance") of this loving fellowship which allowed the Lord to add "to their number day by day those who were being saved" (Acts 2:47).

The Holy Spirit comes to the church for the same purpose that God sent Christ into the world. Paraphrasing John 3:16, we could say, God so loved the world, that he sent the *church*, that the world not perish, but be saved. To prepare and enable the church for just such a task is what happened at Pentecost. The "utterance" made possible by the Spirit does not end with chapter two of Acts or the Day of Pentecost but continues through Acts. In fact, it is characteristic whenever the church is moved by the Spirit of God.

Discussion and Action

1. Read Acts 2 again, focusing on the many ways the Spirit is given "utterance" in the church.
2. Discuss together the ways that you have felt the "coming of the Spirit" in your experience and in your congregation.
3. In the study article, strong emphasis was placed upon the Spirit's giving birth to a church which could take the role of Christ in the world. Do you agree that this is the primary concern in the scripture?
4. How important is the Spirit's witness through the fellowship within your congregation? What could you do to help your congregation's worship and fellowship life become a better witness to Jesus Christ?

2

Healing At The Gate
Acts 3:1-10 (11-26)

Preparation

1. Read quickly Isaiah 35 and 61:1-4, noting the images of "lameness" (weak-kneed, blind, imprisoned, etc.) and why wholeness occurs.
2. Read the text from Acts 3. Note especially the stages in the story and the attitudes associated with each character. What is the connection between what happens in Acts 3 and what you read in Isaiah?

Understanding

Chapter three follows closely upon the events of chapter two. This is more significant theologically than chronologically. Chapter two in Acts had to do with empowering disciples to *be* the body of Christ on earth. The spirit of Christ literally "resurrected" them as God's recreated people. They spent their time rejoicing in that fellowship, nurturing their faith, and celebrating in worship (Acts 2:42).

What we discover in chapter three is that the Spirit of Christ implanted in the body of the church drives us not only to *be* the people of God, but to extend the redemptive hand of Christ to the world God loves. Increased attendance at Temple worship is not the end of the Pentecost rebirth.

Peter and John were on their way to worship at the hour of prayer—about three in the afternoon—when they encountered a lame man. Without health insurance, social security, or county welfare begging was part of the system for caring for the poor and the lame.

The image of the lame man at the gate of the Temple grips me. I can see him there while those going to worship stream by, scarcely aware of his presence. How many lame persons lie at the beautiful gates of our temples? One Sunday morning a man called me with a problem. "My wife and I were living with my mother, but we got kicked out of the house. Can you help us any?" But I was busy with preparing for worship and I was hardly interested in listening to his problem.

I once heard of a pastor who wrapped himself in bandages and tattered clothes one Sunday morning. Then he placed himself right at the foot of the wide stairway leading into the sanctuary. A few didn't notice him. But most made great effort to avoid him. Several even slipped around to the back door in order to enter worship. Some, I suppose, were disgusted that such a person had been allowed near the very gate of their temple. What must the contented worshipers have thought when the pastor came to the pulpit, still unwinding bandages. Surely they realized now quite forcefully that their relationship to the beggar at the gate had much to do with their worship.

Might God be more concerned with what goes on at the gate than with what occurs inside?

It is not only the worshipers but also those at the gate who do not pay attention to persons. "Look at us," Peter and John said. "Look us in the eye." To the beggar, those who passed by were only almsgivers. The beggar gave them opportunity to perform their religious duty to give alms. He played his part, pitifully but absent-mindedly crying, "Alms, alms." Temple-goers threw a coin or two with little actual awareness of his presence.

"Look at us." Peter and John broke through that impersonal haze with a personal word and a personal gaze. Eye contact seems one of the most intimate of human actions. Establishing eye contact immediately draws mere observers into a more personal relationship. Peter and John began to establish a *human* relationship.

Elizabeth O'Connor from the Church of the Savior in Washington, D.C. tells how they learned about the need for human relationship. When the church sought to help the poor in Washington, they learned that providing silver or gold was not their first task. Establishing a relationship was. Instead of first designing programs for the poor, they organized Bible studies in which members of the church and people considered to be poor participated together. They shared with each other, studied with each other, and prayed with each other. They became human beings to each other.

Too often almsgiving, whether in governmental programs or church initiatives, depersonalizes both the giver and the receiver. But people impelled by the Spirit of Christ each personalize and humanize welfare.

The beggar at the gate that day did not get what he expected. No doubt he was quite willing to look at Peter and John, because they might have made a generous gift. He expected wealth, not "wholth." While his lot in life was not great, at least he had a place. Being carried to the Temple, begging for alms, being carried home at dusk—that was his lifestyle. He didn't really expect to change it. He only expected silver or gold.

Instead, Peter and John said, "We don't have what you think you want. But we will give you freely what we do have. In the name of Jesus Christ of Nazareth, walk!" And he did. This paralyzed man was suddenly able to walk, to run, to jump, and, most importantly, to go with them into the Temple. Always before he had come to prey, not to pray. Now the personal touch of Peter and John had brought him into relationship with the God of the universe.

Let's pause for a little word study. The new Testament word for "healing" (*soteria*) is also the word for "salvation." That's why there is so much interplay between healing and salvation, between being made whole and being made right with God. "Salvation" comes from a Latin word *salvus*, meaning health. Zacchaeus restored money to the poor and in that act became whole again and salvation came to his house. Wholeness and salvation went together. Recall the images from Isaiah of the lame and the outcast who leap in joy as they enter the Temple to pray and rejoice. This lame man made whole was able to go into the Temple with Peter and John.

Think a bit about the meaning of temple. "Temple" means a place to meet God. We all know the Temple was in Jerusalem. But in the New Testament the location shifts figuratively to the "people of God." We are the Temple (Eph. 2:20-22; 1 Pet. 2:4-10). In joining us together, God is creating a place where persons can meet the Holy.

What is happening in this passage is that the lame man outside the gate has been taken by the hand and lifted up so that he might enter not just a new *place* but a new *body*, a new people. In that new body, he becomes a new person, healthy and whole. The Church of Jesus Christ has the power to make whole. That's at the heart of this chapter.

Still, there is something else. Much space is given to the *reaction* to the healing. This story in Acts, like others in the New Testament,

may be probing a kind of unrecognized lameness in those who think
that they have entered the temple for worship but have spiritually
remained at the gate, begging for alms.

If we are such persons, we lie at the gate, expecting a return but
never making a contribution. We beg for status, we expect our religion
to give us entry into a certain kind of society, we beg for an identity,
we expect our religion to keep food on the table, but we never have
anything to give. We need to hear loving members of the church saying
"look at us," so that we see in them the face of Jesus Christ as they
extend a hand to us. That can convert us from begging to offering others
the personally experienced riches of Christ.

There is so much lameness in our world. The church is steward
of the power to lift the world. The church has the power to change the
world. We need to take up that challenge in the power of Jesus Christ.
The world needs that even more than silver and gold.

I was gripped by the image of the beggar at the very gate of the
temple. But I guess I was struck more powerfully by the healing at the
gate through a church moved by the Spirit of Christ.

Discussion and Action

1. That "healing" and "salvation" are used to translate the same
   word in the New Testament is a powerful thought. a) How is
   this unity expressed in the story of Zacchaeus? the Good
   Samaritan? Isaiah 53? b) How is it with you? Has your
   salvation come through healing?

2. Discuss the notion that there are persons "begging" at the
   "gates" of our places of worship. Talk about the various kinds
   of persons and how your church, or even your group, might
   be able to extend the uplifting hand of Christ to them.

3. Are there ways in which you lie "at the gate" and need the
   healing that brothers and sisters in the church can offer you?
   Share as much as you feel able about things that keep you from
   entering fully and freely into the life and worship of the
   congregation, and, if it is appropriate, pray for each other's
   wholeness.

4. Is your church a healing fellowship? Share ways that healing
   and wholeness have come to members of your fellowship or
   to you. How can your group produce more "saving wholeness" in your fellowship and for people "at the gate."

3

"They Also Serve ... Who Only Wait On Tables!"

Acts 6:1-7

Preparation

1. Study carefully Acts 6:1-7. Why do you think this story is included in Acts?
2. Read Exodus 18:11-27, noting especially the impact good organization had on the future and the health of Moses and his people.

Understanding

Most of us consider the administrative side of things in the church a bit on the underside of interesting. Acts 6:1-7 may force us to rethink that.

In our study of Acts so far, we have seen the church growing in numbers daily and dramatically. Very quickly, the church had grown from just a few persons to a group numbering in the thousands. Growth brings problems that have to be faced.

At first, the breaking of bread and going to the Temple to rejoice and pray occupied the church. Now, Acts 6:1-7 suggests, the early Christians began to realize that they needed to give their attention to some concerns about the way they did things together.

In particular, the scripture says, the Hellenists began to "murmur" against the Hebrews. "Murmuring" is that background muttering that goes on when some feel put upon by those in charge. It's not focused complaining, just mumbling and stirring up dissent.

Who were the "Hellenists"? The Hellenists were Jews who had grown up in Greek culture and language, rather than Aramaic or Hebrew. They sounded different. Their lifestyles were different, their dress was different, their concerns were different. The Hebrews, on the other hand, were hometown Jews. They had grown up in Palestine. They lived and dressed as good Jews should and prided themselves on the fact that they spoke the right language and obeyed the law with utmost rigor. They were the conservatives. The Hellenists were the liberals.

The Temple, for the Hebrews, was central. We have already noticed that much of the religious life of the early Christians in Jerusalem centered on the Temple and worshiping the Temple. The Hellenists may have been more willing to believe that the Temple building might be destroyed someday.

Becoming Christian did not just wash away those theological and cultural differences. The issue which brought matters to a head, however, was evidently more practical in nature: widows. Evidently, the hometown Hebrews had the charity situation well in hand and the widows were well cared for by the church, aided by sons and daughters who lived in Jerusalem. It was different with the Hellenist widows. The reason is this. Elderly Hellenist Jewish men sometimes moved back to Jerusalem in order to die and be buried near the Holy City. When they died, they left widows. These widows were usually far from family and children, and often impoverished.

The church was making an effort to care for all widows using a practice carried over from the synagogue called "basket and tray." Two collectors went round the market and the private houses every Friday morning and made a collection for the needy partly in money and partly in goods. Later in the day this was distributed. Those who were temporarily in need received enough to enable them to carry on; and those who were permanently unable to support themselves received enough for fourteen meals, that is, enough for two meals a day for the coming week. The fund from which this distribution was made was called the *Kuppah* or Basket. In addition to this a house-to-house collection was made daily for those in pressing need. This was called the *Tamhui*, or Tray (William Barclay, *The Acts of the Apostles: Revised Edition*. Philadelphia: Westminster Press, 1976, p. 51).

Now, the Hebrews in leadership, it seemed to the Hellenists, tended to know of concerns among Hebrew widows much more quickly than among Hellenist ones. But with Hebrew Christians in charge of everything about the church, there was little the Hellenist Christians could do but grumble and murmur. Antagonism threatened to engulf the church and absorb the energy of the leaders.

Something had to be done. The leaders called a meeting. According to the scripture, the Apostles stated the problem this way: "It is not right that we should give up preaching the word of God to serve tables" (Acts 6:2). On the face of it, we might suppose the Apostles were complaining that it was beneath the dignity of preachers to wait tables! Not at all. The matter really has to do with conflict between ministry of table and ministry of word (Acts 6:4). Thus, we could better state the problem for the Apostles, "We should not serve the table, when we should serve the word."

There's more. The word translated "ministry" here is the word from which we get "deacon." In ordinary language the word means something like "to serve," "to wait on people," or even "to wait on tables." The term was also associated with the money changer's "table." Putting all this together, we see that the Apostles were saying, "It isn't right that handling the charitable distribution of wealth and goods should keep us from the work to which we have been called."

If the church had not been willing to deal with this problem by reorganizing itself, we would never have heard of the gospel. Most organizations, with good and noble purposes, get started in order to change the world. Before long, however, the concerns of the organization begin to sap the energy and creativity of leaders. Mission-focus becomes an institution-focus. Does that ever happen in local churches? The continued growth and outreach of the church today depends upon the willingness of leaders to face organizational needs creatively.

The Apostles headed off organizational problems in the early church. First of all, they refused to yield to the temptation that only they could handle anything which needed to be done.

We might note, also, something which did *not* happen. The Apostles did not choose to call the church together and say, "We've heard a lot of bickering going on. It's interfering with our work and we don't have time to deal with it. So stop it right now. Real Christians should not be acting this way." They did not try to convert an organizational problem into a "spiritual" one. That never works.

But there were spiritual consequences. For one thing, the church grew because the preaching of the word of God increased (Acts 6:7). Also, new leaders were called and that had tremendous impact on the future of the church.

The Apostles proposed the selection of seven to take care of what the Apostles should not. Note something very important. The names of those selected were all Hellenistic. They were all persons from the very group that seemed to have been getting the short end.

The early church was actually "Hebrew." The leaders were Jewish, the location was Jewish, the language was Jewish, even "messiah" was a Jewish notion. The major growth and expansion of the church came only when it was able to break out of that mold with a world vision. Not the Hebrew, but the Hellenist Christians were the ones with that vision.

The church may have called them out as leaders to deal with the economic problems of the Jerusalem church, but one of them, Stephen, is not "waiting tables," he is serving in "the ministry of the word." Stephen, obviously well thought of by the congregation, full of the Spirit and wisdom, needed the legitimacy of the divine call through the church. Now he could properly be listened to. And what an impact he and others like him have had.

The ability of the church to fulfill its mission comes not only from preaching and evangelism, not only from increasing in the knowledge and grace of the Lord Jesus, but also from an organizational structure freeing the church to fulfill its ordained task.

Discussion and Action

1. How do you look upon "organization" in your congregation? Is it a vehicle for the growth of the congregation? Is it a bother?

2. Can you give an example of a concern in your congregation which has been met by an organizational change? Do you see some which *could* be changed?

3. What do you think happens when persons, groups, certain families are not treated fairly in the church? How should this be dealt with?

4. Do you ever feel you are able to give leadership in the church where it is most helpful and leads to the most growth—in you and in the church?

5. Do you think differences—cultural, theological, ethnic—can be dealt with organizationally? Is the scriptural example of selecting leaders from disaffected groups a good one? In what situations?

4

"When You Care Enough . . . "
Acts 13:1-3; Acts 20:36—21:6

Preparation

1. Study carefully the passages from Acts 13:1-3; 20:36—21:6. How were Barnabas and Saul "set apart"? Do you think this was the first time that the congregation ever thought of mission work? Or was it a concern with which they had been dealing? Do you find any hints of that in the scripture? What impact did the availability of several prophets and teachers have on the decision?
2. You may want to do a brief study of Paul's letters, looking for passages which suggest his relationship to the believers in various places. Make a list of the passages you find. How important do you think these relationships were?
3. What were the factors which brought you to Christ and the church? Make a few notes about them. Pick out what seems to have had the most effect.

Understanding

"When you care enough . . . " reminds us of a particular brand of greeting card, of course. But it also puts us in the proper context for considering the mission and evangelism of the church. The church is in the business of sending people out. And that action is always rooted in caring, stemming from worship that "sets apart" and commissions.

Christ left the disciples with the assurance that "as the Father has sent me, so I send you" (John 20:21). This means, first of all, that the church, empowered with the Spirit of Christ, has the very same mission as Christ had. The Christian church is sent with the same authority and task as was Christ's. God's sending of Christ is rooted in caring, in love (John 3:16). That mission is always discovered and rooted in worship that "sets apart." The church sends out its own "very best" to accomplish that mission.

What is the worship that sets us apart? First of all, it is worship within the *body* of Christ. In the scriptures we read for this lesson, and throughout the reports of the missionary journeys (Acts 13:1—21:14), the impressive thing is the tender and deep fellowship Paul had with the congregations which developed. It appears that the relationships established were just as important as the words said in the development of new church fellowships. Caring, rooted in God's care for us, is one of the most powerful motives for evangelizing. Its power to attract is even stronger.

Win Arn, well known in American Church Growth circles, wrote recently that those in our day who are "hungry for the gospel" are not hungry for content-oriented presentations, either on TV or in person. Arn contends that modern social scientists and anthropologists are saying increasingly that love (friendship, relationship) is and will be the predominant concern of our culture well into the 1990s. Although the image of love in our culture is badly warped, the need for love is part of every human being and can find its fulfillment only in the love of God, he says. Then he adds, "Evangelizing America—the world— will be effective in direct relationship to the church's ability to evidence Christ's love."

Obviously, we may miss something terribly significant about Paul's missionary work, if we focus merely on the words that he carried and ignore the fellowship that he created. By the same token, we will miss the center of our evangelistic opportunity if we fail to see the building of community as part and parcel of the ministry of the word.

We may need to change our vision. A change of vision is not easy. When I was in seminary, many of the wives taught in suburban schools. In the winter time, when the snow was deep on the Chicago streets, deep ruts developed. There were two in the parking lane on both sides of the street and then a single lane of ruts down the center of the street. The high ridges between the sets of ruts made it difficult either to get into the parking lane or into traffic. Each morning we had to be on hand to get the cars out into the ruts in the road and back again in the evening into the parking ruts. That may parallel the situation for many of us with respect to our view about evangelism. It's hard to *change* ruts—

whether of customary practice or of vision. It takes help, presence, leadership, and effort to change ruts.

The second thing that needs to be said about "worship that sets apart" is that it is based on the call of God. Being sent out always begins with God's call. Grace is at God's initiative. God came first to us, not we to God. That means both our worship and our evangelism is at God's invitation.

Why did the Antioch church choose to set apart Barnabas and Paul? We might say simply, as the scripture does, that the Holy Spirit told them to. They recognized in them a call of God that the church needed to confirm. "Set apart for me Barnabas and Saul for the work to which I have called them" (Acts 13:2). If the call of God was clear, wasn't that enough? Why did the church need to add its blessing? The community of the Spirit, the covenant community, mediates the blessing of God, confirms the word of God, and affirms the direction of God's work in the world.

Frank Tillapaugh has a helpful perspective. He uses the concept of "unleashing people for ministry." Churches, he says, tend to become "event-oriented." We must become "strategy-oriented." We must stop asking "What can we do?" and begin to ask "What does the Lord want us to accomplish?" Too often, we are more concerned with getting people onto committees than into ministry. The church at Antioch was "unleashing" Barnabas and Paul. We need to do something similar with the work of nominating committees and commissions if our congregation is to grow in life and mission.

When we call persons for a task or to assume a role, we need to think in terms of *releasing* them to do the work to which the Holy Spirit has called them, rather than of tying them down. It's not just a question of "who will do it?" but "who is called to do it?" The concept of the "body" implies that not all will have the same tasks or opportunities. Some in the congregation are more the "visionaries" who are able to dream boldly about new ways to serve God. Others are more the "administrators" who can take those bold dreams and figure out a way to make them happen, making the difficult decisions and figuring out where to find the resources. Some seem to be gifted as "workers," who, when given proper training and authority to do the task, can carry through an assignment well. All are needed for the growth of the church. What a miracle that Barnabas was not assigned to the table committee in Antioch simply because someone had to do it!

Strangely enough, even the Hindu Ghandi agreed with Win Arn's estimate of the importance of "love" in evangelism. E. Stanley Jones, the famous Christian missionary to India, once reported on a chance meeting with Ghandi, when they both found themselves lodged for the night in the same guesthouse. At the time Ghandi was becoming known for fighting imperialism and struggling for independence. Jones asked whether Ghandi would have men like Jones leave India. What Ghandi suggested instead was a philosophy of mission: Christian missionaries should 1) make love primary, 2) live their religion—put it into practice, 3) be clear about what they believe so that Indians can understand it, and 4) be more understanding of other religions. Is there any reason why this should not apply to all our efforts to spread the gospel?

Do we care enough to send . . . ?

Discussion and Action

1. Reflect on some past meaningful worship experiences in your congregation or your covenant group. Does worship in your congregation tend to lead to the "unleashing" of leaders?
2. Do the leaders in your group or congregation see beyond your local congregation? Or are you satisfied that the real work is at home?
3. Think about the way persons are selected for leadership in your congregation. Do you think there is more concern about getting people onto committees than into ministry? Are there ways you and your group could help to change that pattern?
4. Reflect on the offices and the persons in leadership roles of all kinds in your congregation. What percentage of the leadership has a task or role directed in any way toward evangelism and helping the church to grow? 50% 25% 10% 1.3%? Since we tend to accomplish what we spend time doing, are there ways you could help increase the number of persons working to help your church reach out to new persons?

5

"Light For The Road"
Acts 9:1-19a

Preparation

1. Study carefully the story of the Apostle Paul's conversion in Acts 9:1-19a. Compare the accounts in Acts 22:4-16 and Acts 26:9-18. Look at Paul's own rendering in Galatians 1:11-24. Note particularly the progression from one account to another and the outcome for Paul.
2. After you look at the story of Paul's conversion, look at a writing from a later time, such as 1 Corinthians 12-14. How can his emphasis there relate to Paul's experience with Ananias and through him, with the church?

Understanding

This little story of the Apostle Paul's conversion may well be the most famous conversion story in history. Most of us not only know the story but have struggled with it as well.

We too often miss the point of the story because we look at it as an experience that will move us to right action. But we miss the way in which this very personal event for Paul can also become, perhaps in an entirely different way, an equally personal encounter with the risen Christ on the road that we follow.

So, let's look at the story. Paul was causing great havoc in the church. The Sanhedrin assigned Saul, as he was called among Hebrews, to rid Jerusalem of a group following one they proclaimed as the Messiah.

One reason that such a proclamation was disturbing to Paul the Jew was that proclaiming someone the "anointed king" fit a pattern of rebelliousness that the Romans feared so much in Judea. This was just one more unsettling influence that could bring the Romans down on the necks of the Jews. Even more than that, it seemed contrary to what Paul had learned in his training as a good Pharisee. The Christians seemed to be putting the Law in second place and the Temple in third.

Thus, Paul set out to rid Jerusalem, indeed the whole world, of those "Christians." I suspect that every time he went into a house to drag out a Christian, every time he forced them to renounce their faith, he must have been moved deeply by the quality of their faith and the intensity of their devotion. But even more he was moved by the way Christians responded to his violent approach to them. Perhaps they responded as Christ had responded to his torturers: "Father, forgive him, for he knows not what he does."

So here is Paul on his way to Damascus with the authority to find every Christian who had fled Jerusalem, to tie them up, and to take them back to Jerusalem to certain torture and probable death. Paul traveled to Damascus on foot. It takes about six days to walk 140 miles. And he was alone except, perhaps, for Temple police. But Paul was a strict Pharisee, he would have had little to do with such persons.

So Paul, fresh from a frenzied effort in Jerusalem to hunt down and kill every Christian, is now on his way to Damascus, walking by himself for six days with dust in his nostrils, the sun beating down on his head, and the sounds of the persecution ringing in his ears. Likely, the closer he got to Damascus, the more the turmoil raged within. Before he could reach Damascus, however, he was struck down on the road. Struck down with light.

That simple event had earth-shaking significance. A light from heaven flashed around him and said, "Saul, why are you persecuting me?" Now, the question doesn't seem right. Paul wasn't persecuting Christ. He was killing Christians. Hidden in the form of this question, you see, is an insight which becomes central to Paul. The person of Christ is identified with his body the church! To persecute Christ's followers is to persecute Christ.

Later on, that identity is at the center of Paul's thinking. In his writings it is often difficult to distinguish between Christ and the church. When Paul says, "In Christ," he often means clearly, "in the body of Christ, his church." To be "in Christ" is to be a "member" of his body. So the question, "Why are you persecuting me?" was a blinding insight about the nature of Christianity. In fact the whole experience is directed toward that profound revelation.

Then the voice of the Lord says, "Go into Damascus and there you will be told what to do." Why didn't Christ just get it over with on the road? Why didn't the voice say, "Paul, here is what I want you to do. You are to be my person. Go to the Gentiles with the message of Jesus." Wouldn't that have been simpler?

Instead, Christ sends Paul into town to find out the next step. The next days were the worst days of Paul's life. Three days alone. Couldn't sleep, couldn't eat, couldn't see a thing. Three days in darkness. A time to be dead and reborn. Still the risen Christ did not come to Paul and say, "Okay! This is what I want you to do."

To Paul the Lord sent Ananias, a member of the very body whom Paul had been persecuting. That is, the Lord sent the "persecutee" to Paul the "persecutor" with a message wrapped up in the very first words Ananias spoke, *"Brother* Saul." In that simple phrase the whole gospel came with enlightening power to blinded Paul. Hateful Paul was touched with loving grace by a member of the church. The love, the acceptance, the grace, and the mercy that Paul met through Ananias redeemed Paul. "Let me show you," he writes later, "a still more excellent way" (1 Cor. 12:31b). He knew exactly what he was talking about.

How important it is for simple, ordinary members of the church to be ready to respond with the word and with the life of acceptance and redemption as Ananias did. Again and again the vulnerable Paul was dependent upon others for his life. After this experience in Damascus, Paul was still hated and feared. Christians still ran when they saw him coming. Barnabas, a good man, brought Paul to the church and vouched for him, so that Paul could go in and out among the members and they could be strengthened by his ministry. It was also Barnabas who got Paul in the right place for ministry by first bringing Paul to Antioch. Ananias, Barnabas, Stephen, Silas, Timothy, and many others were the ones through whom the word of God came in a way that gave Paul light for the road.

A husband and wife once visited an orphanage. They wanted to adopt a child. In glowing terms they told the chosen boy about the many things they could provide for him. To their amazement, the little fellow responded, "Well, if you have nothing to offer except a good home, clothes, toys and other things most kids have, I would just as soon stay here in the orphanage." Their mouths dropped open. "What more could you possibly want?" Said the little boy, "I just want someone to love me."

The boy simply wanted people to draw him into the human family. That was precisely what Paul received from the church he had persecuted. Is it not also what draws us into the church? We have heard the voice of God when persons have touched us with the very hands of Christ. What could happen to us on a Damascus road as we begin to hear the voice of God through our experiences and through the persons who touch us with the hands of Christ?

One thing that can happen is that we receive a sense of being *chosen*. It is not our emotions, our intellect, or the depth of our commitment, but the abiding sense that God has reached out and touched you and me and said, "You are the one. I want you." There is also the sense of being *directed*. We no longer go our way, but God's way. We also know a sense of being *protected*. Paul's writings detail the suffering he experienced. Yet, we *can* say that Paul was protected. We can have the same sense of protection. Romans 8:34ff. says it all: in spite of everything and anything that happens, Paul writes, he is sure that nothing can separate him "from the love of God in Christ Jesus, my Lord." That love came first through the touch of Ananias' hand. Paul knew that love could not be taken away.

Touched, chosen, directed, protected—may God open our eyes, too, with that kind of vision.

Discussion and Action

1. In this treatment of Paul's conversion is the idea that the most redemptive impact of Christ on a person comes through the life and outreach of the congregation. Can you think of other stories in your faith experience and the experience of your congregation or Covenant group which bear that out?

2. Discuss the various aspects of Paul's conversion. How does it compare with your own understanding and experience? Has the study of this session given you any new perspectives?

3. Discuss John 13:34-35 in relation to evangelism, conversion, and the life of your covenant group. Are there ways that your group could become more contagiously evangelistic?

6

The Push To Include
Acts 10:9-48

Preparation

1. Study Acts 10:9-48. Note the progression of Peter's understanding.
2. Read Isaiah 42:1-4; 49:6. What meaning do you think these texts have for the mission of the church?

Understanding

From the Day of Pentecost, there has been constant missionary pressure. Yet, a little between-the-lines reading shows that the early church and its leaders were really "caged in" by the notion that the message "Jesus is the Christ" was a message *for* Jews alone. It is clear, however, that God intended from the beginning that the word be for all peoples everywhere.

Many Jews who heard and believed the good news of Christ felt that, while others might be drawn to believe, it was still a story for Jews. It was a story about their faith, about God working to redeem all creation through a chosen people. That noble structure became a cage from which the church might never have escaped, had not God broken down the doors.

The scripture itself was clearer than many wanted to admit. There were passages like Isaiah 42:17. This passage speaks of the Messiah, but in speaking of the Messiah, it speaks of the role of the church to carry on the task of the Messiah and be Christ's presence for our day. Even clear statements of God's agenda, however, can be used to wall out the ones God is attempting to reach.

But God has a way of breaking such cages. Stephen, once he was called to leadership in the church (see Session Three), began to speak a disturbing word. "The gospel was for Gentiles, too! That was God's intention from the beginning," he said. To say that God *wanted* Gentiles included in the fold seemed to be a heresy that could not be tolerated.

We might too quickly jump to the conclusion from what we read in Acts that God simply rejected the Jews and turned to the Gentiles. Even the Apostle Paul agonizes in Romans 9—11 over what seems to be a rejection of God's former people, the Jews, and a turning to Gentiles. Paul seems to say that in God's way of working, the *apparent* rejection of the Jews and acceptance of the Gentiles was actually having the effect of making the Jews jealous enough to want to be drawn in. So, the net effect was that Jew and Gentile inherited the kingdom together. The push to include was at the heart of the matter on God's agenda—and still is.

Peter's personal struggle personifies the struggle for the whole church. In chapter ten we see Peter, in Joppa, visiting with Simon the Tanner. Even though he was a Jew, Simon was *unclean* because he handled carcasses. The other Simon, Peter, was a good, *clean* Jew who felt that being God's person meant following God's laws. Avoiding uncleanness was very important. But here he was, in the home of Simon. Evidently Simon was a Christian so Peter knew they ought to be brothers. Yet, should he really eat food prepared in this tanner's house? It is in eating together that we most clearly demonstrate our being family. Yet, to eat with someone who is unclean was a sin.

While Peter meditated, something like a great sheet came down from heaven containing all kinds of animals. Then a demanding, heavenly voice said, "Peter, you are hungry. Kill and eat." When Peter looked he saw not only the cows he should eat but the pigs he shouldn't eat. In horror he drew back, "Sir, I have never let anything unclean cross my lips and I am not about to now just because I'm hungry." The heavenly voice was persistent. "Peter, what I have declared clean you must not call common."

Remember the story of Jesus telling the disciples what kind of Messiah he would be, how he would suffer and die. Again it was Peter who tried to correct God's Christ! "No, no, that is not how it should go." So Jesus had to correct Peter, "Peter, you are like a satan. You are a hindrance when you try to lead me; you must follow me" (Mark 8:27ff.). Peter had the same reaction in Acts. He thought he knew the Law well enough to correct the voice of the Lord! Something more important than food was at stake here. It was even more fundamental than hesitancy to eat with the tanner. It had to do with God's agenda of declaring all people clean and acceptable.

Then a prompting of the Spirit told Peter that some Gentiles were coming and he should accept them without question. He would normally have had no fellowship with Gentiles. But now he believed that God was moving him to accept them. And he did accept them, brought them into the house, and offered them lodging. He even ate with them. He accepted the invitation to go with them, as he felt God was prompting him to do. Finally, the point was more clear.

So, when Peter addressed the friends and relatives the centurion Cornelius had assembled, he said, "You know that I normally wouldn't be here. It is beyond human imagination to think that I, a Jew, would be found in this house. But God has shown me that anyone anywhere, not just Jews, but anyone with the right mind and heart can rightly hear the good news. Therefore, I am not embarrassed to be here or to tell you the whole gospel story." Then, to his surprise, the very same thing happened to the Gentiles that had happened to the Jews assembled in the upper room at Pentecost. They received the Holy Spirit. The sign of God's presence overcoming them showed in their faces, in their lives, in their actions and words. For Peter, the conclusion was now crystal clear. "If God has chosen them and poured the Spirit out on them, how can we but accept them into the fellowship, baptize them, and declare them humanly clean, just as God has done." Hardly believing what was happening, they baptized them.

Word of what had happened arrived in Jerusalem before the party returned, and Peter was called on the carpet immediately. Was it true? Did he actually preach to Gentiles? Peter simply told what had happened. When the leaders of the church in Jerusalem heard the story they gulped, but they confirmed Peter's judgment. "If God has chosen to grant them the kind of repentance that will give them life in Christ, then who are we to stand in the way of God?" (Acts 11:17-18) Indeed!

Still, it wasn't always a happy story from then on. I suppose the reason the story is told so carefully and the report of Peter's heavenly vision is repeated at least three times, is simply that it was a hard point to get across.

Has it gotten across yet? God wants to lead us into Gentile territory. Gentiles are those people who we say are not God's chosen people. More accurately, they are not part of *our* chosen few. They're those who don't feel at home here, who really aren't our kind. I wonder if we don't fall into assuming the gospel is for those who are like us, who know the way things happen around here. Our good news is for those trained to get up early Sunday morning, put on good clothes, rush around to get all the kids ready in time to hurry to church in order to sit in one spot without moving, while struggling to keep the kids quiet.

What makes one eligible to be a Christian? We may think that being "one of us" is necessary. But God prepares persons in many places. The great surprise is that God intends for the message of Christ to be heard far beyond the realm of those who seem most prepared for it by background.

Do we resist the revelation that, "It isn't just something nice I'm doing for you. I want to make you a light for all people so that my wholeness can become life for all"? Perhaps we, like Peter, need to experience God urging us to accept those with whom we don't feel comfortable. People who don't act, dress, or have the same values as we do can, nevertheless, become brothers and sisters in the family of God. When we allow that to happen, we too may be surprised by a "Gentile Pentecost," when God demonstrates their acceptance as children.

Discussion and Action

1. Does our situation in life affect how we interpret scripture? Discuss ways that might happen.
2. Are there people who are "unclean" for us? You may want to share personal difficulties in accepting certain persons into your congregation or even into your group. How can we grow in inclusiveness skills?
3. Clearly, in the story in Acts, the Gentiles were more ready to hear the gospel than were the Jews. How can we be open to those in our culture who are ready to hear and respond to the Christian faith, even though they don't have church background? Where and how do we find them?
4. Some of the dearest tenets of faith in the early church had to undergo change in order for "dividing walls" to be broken down. Do you have some ideas that need to change before your congregation can become truly open to folks God wants to reach through you?

7

The Push To Divide
Acts 15:(1-35), 36-41

Preparation

1. Try to look at Acts 15 with fresh eyes. Read it aloud, record it and play it back, outline it. Note all the viewpoints, the decisions, the characters.
2. Study Galatians 2 for Paul's viewpoint on the issue of the Jerusalem Council.

Understanding

With the kind of membership the early church had, the drive toward division was great. But the gospel has within it a powerful dynamic that draws people together, making one. That dynamic is love, the divine movement of God in Christ, overcoming barriers and divisions within creation, destroying that which antagonizes by drawing together and creating one "flesh" (Col. 1:15-20).

Since love is so fundamental to faith, issues between groups or persons could not be left to fester. Acts 15 shows the struggle to deal with and come to some agreement about these issues. It also portrays how the church began to develop an identity separate from Judaism. Especially at Antioch various elements of the Christian church began to come together. In that struggle the separate identity began to develop. That the "followers of the Way" were first called "Christians" at Antioch (Acts 11:26) was a recognition of this new identity.

The earliest Christians considered themselves Jews. In their minds, the Messiah, long expected by the Jews, had come. As persons who weren't really Jews heard and responded to that gospel and God confirmed their standing by pouring out the Spirit upon them as well, a confusing situation was created. What was the status of those who were not Jews but still had been accepted by God? How could non-Jews be one with Jews in their response to the coming of God's Messiah?

To some believers, the solution was self-evident. Outsiders should become good Jews. That meant first of all, they should be *circumcised*. If God wants non-Jews, it has to mean that God must want them to be circumcised as well. If they have been chosen, they should show that in the flesh.

The issue here was not really making them Jews. The issue was unity in the church, "table fellowship." The church needed to eat together at the table of the Lord, the Love Feast, the koinonia meal. Believers among the Pharisees were finding it particularly difficult to eat with Christians of pagan background. But the problem would be solved, they thought, if circumcision made them real Jews. For too many years the ungodly had been referred to as the "uncircumcised."

Peter and others had been delighted at first by the new life among the Gentiles at Antioch and were happy to sit down with them to eat. Very soon, however, believers from Jerusalem said: "They have to be circumcised. We have to be loyal to the tradition in which God has called us and trained us. We have to tell them to obey the Law of Moses. They can't be saved unless they do. Furthermore, it's necessary if we are to be one body, with one faith, and one Lord."

Peter and Barnabas were moved by this line of argument. The uncircumcised Christians, however, were not and refused to be circumcised. Two groups began to form. The Jews ate one agape-koinonia meal, non-Jews another. But no one was satisfied. Paul was horrified. He rightly recognized that this practice was no compromise. It struck at the very heart of the gospel and would eventually destroy the church if allowed to continue.

Why not two churches? Why not a Jewish church to attract the Pharisees, a pagan-Christian church for the Gentiles? One in which you had to be circumcised and obey the Law of Moses and one in which you didn't? Something for everyone! Differences, we must admit, have often led to outreach and growth. The split between Paul and Barnabas led to *two* missionary journeys where there would otherwise have been only one. Again and again throughout church history, divisions seem to have allowed growth and persons to be reached for Christ and the church. Why not be satisfied with that?

God never blesses division and separation as such. True, God may be able to use divisions and splits to make the church grow, but God never gives the final blessing to that. The fundamental push of the faith is toward unity. We really have no choice, for instance, about the ecumenical movement. We must continue to work at church fellowships becoming one. As long as we are separated, the need to find ways to draw us together is urgent.

Therefore, "you go your way and I'll go mine" was not acceptable in Antioch. The issue needed to be settled, so the Antiochan church sent leaders to Jerusalem. Why Jerusalem? Because they were looking toward a decision that would bring unity, not simply for freedom to do it their own way. If a decision were made in Antioch the church would be split. So they went to where the decision needed to be made and where, once made, it would draw the church together.

The conference in Jerusalem was not calm, but it got to the heart of the matter. Through strong, loving interaction and with the Spirit's work, the body came to see how completely the action of God in Christ had changed their relationship to the Law of Moses.

When it came time for a decision, I think they voted. I think there were tears as well as shouts and embracing when the vote was clear. I'm sure, too, that they believed it was not just their own vote but the recognition of what the Spirit had accomplished to help them see something new. With that decision came a recognition of the distinctive identity of the *Christian Church* as well. They decided that both Jew and Gentile are saved by the grace of God and not by any action of their own, not even circumcision, no matter how different in custom, in tradition, in habit. We are made one by the grace of God in Christ. It meant that both Jew and Gentile are one in Christ, not two.

That settled, they were able to begin to deal with the practical questions of getting along. Issues of unity are seldom purely theological. Usually it's body odor, the slant of the eye, the custom of dress, or standard of values. The four things which were to be asked of the Gentiles were more like basic rules for getting along so that Jews could handle fellowship with them. It certainly was not a new Law of Moses which had to be strictly adhered to.

Why talk about circumcision? That's not a problem in anybody's church. But the "Judaizing spirit" is. That, sadly enough, has never left us. God accepts unconditionally. We never seem to.

Most of us have come to know Christ through our experience in our own denomination. Because it has revealed the love of God to us, that tradition has a holy feel about it. But it is possible for God to reach persons in ways outside a particular tradition. Where God is accepting, we need to accept also, remembering that we are never saved by our obedience to a denomination but always by the God's grace. Dealing with differences may be necessary. But we can respect each other, ultimately, as family. The gospel always drives us to do that. We can never be satisfied with divisions.

At the Alive '85 Conference on Evangelism, Myron Augsburger reported an incident he witnessed at the Congress of Evangelism at Berlin in 1966. In the foyer, he said, two men suddenly confronted each other. One was an Arab pastor, the other a Jewish Christian. They stopped, almost startled, looking at each other.

One blurted, "I saw your people kill my people." The other looked right back and said, "And I saw my people killed by your people." Tension was felt by all in the foyer. All at once they smiled and reaching out put their arms around each other, and Augsburger heard them say, "Isn't it wonderful to know a Christ who makes us one."

Whenever we face concerns that divide our fellowship, we know that we serve a risen Christ who makes us one. Humanly speaking, our task is always to work at discovering that.

Discussion and Action

1. When we resist the temptation to "go our separate ways" and struggle through the issues that divide, a new identity and a deeper relationship always seem to result. Can you share incidents from your experience where this has been true? Incidents from the life of your congregation? Your group?

2. The decision made at Jerusalem in Acts 15 "seemed good to the Holy Spirit and to them." Is that a "principle" for our decision-making? How can we help that to occur? What significance does it have that Antioch met with the Jerusalem church to make a decision about this issue? How does that apply in your congregation? Your group?

3. How does the "Judaizing spirit" show up in a congregation? Have you ever had such a spirit? Been the victim of it? How can it be overcome? Does it ever enter into a Covenant group?

4. How can we handle differences in a way that enhances and protects "table fellowship" while preserving the creativity of diversity?

8

"If You Have The Word, Say It!"
Acts 13:13-16, 26-33a

Preparation

1. Study the scripture passages for this lesson. Note especially the way Paul structures his message to the people at Antioch.
2. Think about how faith in Jesus Christ has come to mean something to you. Jot a few notes about the "story" of faith you have to tell. What experiences is it based on? Scriptures? Ideas? Relationships?

Understanding

When the power goes off, my work in the computer is gone. Just . . . gone! It simply disappears. It is nowhere to be found. I could tear the computer apart, wire by wire, chip by chip, and I would end up with nothing—not even a computer!

When I lose something like that, a kind of despair, even anger, sweeps over me. My strenuous effort seems in vain. Something that I brought into existence for a brief moment on the screen has passed away so quickly. Come to nothing. I am difficult to console.

When that happened to me again a few days ago, I wondered whether that was the source of human anger about the snuffing out of life. Is life no more than a volatile "electronic" memory existing as long as the power is on. We think that should not be true. But we also think that our precious information should not be lost from the computer. Do we not long to hear that there is some kind of permanent saving place for the volatile memory of human life?

There is some consolation about what I have lost from the computer's memory. What was lost from the computer is still in my memory, though never in quite the same form. At times I have discovered to my delight that what I lost and then recovered from *my* own memory was better reworked than before.

But is there consolation for our questions about life itself? Zorba, in *Zorba, the Greek,* asked Boss, "Why do people die? What do all your books tell you about that?" But Boss was unable to answer the question. When Boss tried to tell Zorba why he could not answer the questions, Zorba grew disgusted and angry. What good are all those books, if they don't answer the questions that really matter? Had the answers gotten lost in a computer maze?

When Paul sat down in the synagogue in Antioch of Pisidia, the rulers of the synagogue sent a compelling invitation to Paul, "If you have any word of encouragement for the people, say it." The Jews there, like people in many places, were certainly in need of a word of consolation, a word of encouragement, of hope.

Paul and his party had to struggle to get to Antioch. We should note, first of all, that they were there. They could not have been asked for encouragement, had they not been there. Antioch of Pisidia wasn't the easiest place to get to, either. John Mark took one look at the journey inland and said, "No way. I'm going back to Jerusalem."

Because the local people knew it was a struggle to get there, and because there were no tourists in those days, the local people would have assumed Paul was there for a reason. Traveling was far from easy. There were robbers, there was lack of food, there was disease. Some think Paul might have picked up malaria on this trip. The pains and agonies of malaria could well be a "thorn in the flesh."

So . . . "If you have something encouraging to say, we want to hear it." Indeed he did. When Paul spoke, he referred to the scriptures. In our day, if we are asked to say something important, we usually think we should quote the Bible. Scripture verses!

Remember that the early church did not have the Bible; they had the Scriptures. They didn't have the writings of Paul, the Acts of the Apostles—they had the Scripture.

In our day, when we say "gospel," we usually mean specifically "Matthew, Mark, Luke, or John." When Paul spoke of the gospel, he didn't mean anything literary at all. He didn't mean the book, he meant the message. He didn't have it written, it was incorporated in his own flesh. When we are asked to speak the word, it is not Bible verses, but the word that comes through our own life and discovery which we must speak. That is a "word of encouragement." When we teach like the scribes and the Pharisee who merely quoted from the ancients, our word is seldom a witness. But when it comes through our life, then it is powerful, and speaks a "word of encouragement."

There were three things that Paul emphasized in this scripture. First, the history of God's work that began in the ancient human past is moving through us into a purposeful future. History has meaning and direction. It is not just meaningless cycles. It has purpose and God is behind it. God presides over the story of history, not just of the creation. In the life we live, in our family story, our congregational story, our country's story, God has a purpose.

The next point was that God is faithful. It is especially on this point that Paul was beginning to announce a word of consolation. The word was that God is faithful. Not only does God preside over all, not only is God working through history, but God is faithful. As we watch history we can be consoled that God *will* accomplish a plan. "God is the ruler yet." We can have the confidence that history finally is in God's hands and the plan will be accomplished.

Paul's scripture was a story of fulfillment. He talked the words of David. Every Jew was aware of God's promise to David. The promise was that God would raise up a king out of the house of David to reign forever. God loved David; David was a man after God's own heart. Paul claimed that in Jesus Christ, God had fulfilled promises to David. That says something about history and about the assurance we can have that God will fulfill every promise.

The third part of Paul's message of consolation was that now, through God's faithful action in Jesus, we can receive in ourselves the fulfillment of the promises which God has made. In particular, Paul said, it is a message of salvation and redemption. It is a message of forgiveness. Repentance with forgiveness is not dry gospel but brings new hope. God responds to repentance.

The impact of the prophetic word of the Old Testament to Jews of that day and to us ethical strugglers today is a word of *repentance*. "Change, be different, live like you should!" We hear that word. We struggle. We want to make it. I would like to be different; I would like to do what I ought to do. The announcement that Paul brought was that in Jesus, in the faithful action of God, repentance has not gone unnoticed in God's eyes.

The gospel is power to change. God does not stand far off and say, "Go ahead, try to do better; come on, you can do it." God responds to forgiveness with freedom, the third thing Paul covered. There is freedom for us in the forgiving power of Jesus Christ. Freedom is the ability and capacity to be what God wants us to be. That is a divine gift, not a human possession. Repentance we can struggle at, but for the power to be different, we need God's empowering.

Paul knew that power in his own life and he could announce it. Each time he announced it, persons then and now were and are able to receive it. The consequence is to walk in newness of life, living out in their own lives freedom of the fruits of the Spirit.

A word of encouragement? Indeed it was. Somehow the invitation to Paul on that Sabbath day rings out for us, too. If you have the word of encouragement, you are called upon to say it. First of all, go where the word needs to be heard. Establish relationships. Words are heard out of a relationship that we have with the persons who hear the word. That is why words of condemnation seldom have any effect outside our community. Words of encouragement within the family, within the church, within the fellowship where there is a good relationship have strong effect. Lastly, we need to be able to share the word of consolation that comes out of the discovery of the gospel through our own mind and heart. Go, be there, share. You have the "word of consolation for the people."

Discussion and Action

1. Discuss with your group how you have used scripture in your life. What passages have meant most to you and why?
2. The passage we studied for this lesson referred to the way in which the Apostle Paul used scripture to communicate the gospel. How do you think scripture should be used? Why doesn't "reading them Bible verses" work?
3. What is the gospel for you? If you were asked for a "word of encouragement" for the people, what would you say? What does Christ mean to you?
4. How could you and your group help to share "a word of encouragement" for persons in your community? Paul was *asked* to share his faith. In what situations are you asked to share? How can you be ready to do that? Are there ways you can increase the likelihood that you *will* be asked?

9

"Of One Heart And Soul"
Acts 4:32-37; Acts 11:27-30

Preparation

1. Study carefully the scripture listed. How does "togetherness" manifest itself in the New Testament?
2. Study Acts 4:32-37 with special care. Do you see any connection between the "testimony to the resurrection" and "great grace" upon the church, on the one hand, and the lack of needy persons in the church on the other?

Understanding

The early church was "together" in heart and in soul (Acts 2:44; 4:32). This wholeness in the New Testament church was produced by their resurrection into a new body through the infusion of the Spirit of Christ. They found it true that the more their love for God increased the more they loved their neighbor as themselves. One of the most attractive things about Christians was their new life together. They lived not just as individuals but as a body, together in "heart and soul."

That bond of heart and soul in Christ began to link them with Christians all over the world. One expression of this bonding was an offering for the Jerusalem church from Gentile Christians. Beyond this aid for material poverty, there was a concern about spiritual poverty. Paul speaks, for instance, of encouraging those who are strong to help the weak. That all resulted from and helped to strengthen their being one in heart and soul.

One person in particular, it seems to me, was instrumental in helping to build that oneness, Barnabas. Barnabas, the scripture says simply, was a "good man." I know of no one else referred to in the New Testament as good. Persons are redeemed, made new, are considered faithful servants, but seldom if ever are they referred to as good.

Yet here is Barnabas, a *good* man. Actually, Barnabas wasn't his name; Joseph was. The Apostles gave him the nickname, or surname. Surely, it was meant to describe his character.

The Living Bible calls him "Barny the Preacher." Actually there is some justification for that. The Hebrew would likely mean "son of prophecy." In the New Testament, prophecy is something closer to our word "preaching." Paul considers prophecy more as proclamation of good news, telling of the glory of God. The American Standard Version follows this understanding by calling Barnabas a "son of exhortation."

Usually his nickname is translated "son of consolation" (KJV), or "son of encouragement" (NIV or RSV). Interestingly, the Greek word has the same root as another Greek word that we sometimes use in English: *Paraclete*. That's the word used for Comforter, Helper, Advocate, the Encourager whom Christ will send (John 14:16; 1 Jn. 2:1). That this word is used for Barnabas seems profound.

The scripture suggests that Barnabas is a "son of the Paraclete," of the Encourager. His spirit reflected the Spirit whom Christ had sent. His spirit was moved by the Spirit of the Master Encourager, the Counselor, the Comforter, precisely the Spirit of Jesus.

In Barnabas, the church recognized something profound about the Holy Spirit and the way the Holy Spirit works among the fellowship. When Barnabas heard about the gospel, he responded. Evidently he was transformed by this encounter with the Lord. He did not merely say, "Hey, I'd like to be a member." He came with everything. He even sold a field and gave the proceeds to the apostles to manage. His deed was in marked contrast to the actions of Ananias and Sapphira (Acts 4:36).

More significantly, the Jerusalem church sent him down to Antioch when they heard about the response of the Gentiles. They chose Barnabas because they knew that Barnabas would respond with an open heart and mind. He would be ready to look for what God was doing. He would not accept the prejudice that the word should never have been preached to the Gentiles. They expected Barnabas to be receptive to new ideas.

In Antioch he saw what was happening and he was "glad." Others might have said, "These people don't have the look of good Jews at all. They don't behave right. They don't pronounce Hebrew accurately.

And worst of all, they have Jews and Gentiles eating together at one table." No, Barnabas rejoiced at what was happening and set about to encourage the church.

How important persons like Barnabas are in the church! We need teachers who have the "ear of the learner." Barnabas evidently had that "tongue" and "ear." Thus, he could reflect the very Spirit of the Paraclete. We need to have that same ear. We need people in the congregation who are able to recognize what people are working toward, what their purpose and intention is, and who are able to draw it out.

We need those who can encourage what is growing rather than to merely pick out what is wrong. Children, for instance, are objectively wrong much of the time. But the beauty of parents is that they can see what the child is reaching for, what the child is attempting, and can respond to attempt rather than to the mistakes and inadequacies.

Barnabas' ministry of encouragement proved important not only to the Gentiles in Antioch, but to the Apostle Paul, as well. It was probably Barnabas who introduced Paul into the work which made him more famous than Barnabas. When the missionary work started, the report read "Barnabas and Paul." Then the text changed to "Paul and Barnabas." Soon, Barnabas dropped out of the picture almost entirely. Barnabas was the one who introduced Paul to the Jerusalem church when they were still scared to death of him. It was the encouraging Barnabas who was able to draw Paul in, allay the fears, and encourage the congregation to accept this person so that he could become the leader God intended him to be.

Leaders in the limelight very often find their strength through the encouragement of the congregation they lead. When groups become antagonistic toward leaders and the leaders antagonistic toward the group, the strength is gone. I know a few pastors from whom I didn't expect much. To my surprise they have become good pastors and excellent leaders. I believe it is because of the way their congregations have encouraged them and drawn out the "good pastor" in them.

Well, Barnabas was the kind of person who could develop that spirit in a congregation. He drew Paul into the fellowship at Jerusalem, and then when Barnabas went down to Antioch, he said, "It is clear that God has made Paul to be the kind of person who can serve in this situation," and he went and looked for him. In Antioch, things really began to happen for Paul. It was Barnabas who had the ability to recognize that possibility and to draw it out.

It may well be that each of us is dependent upon "Barnabases" in our own past who have encouraged and supported us. They may have been Sunday school teachers, committee chairpersons, counselors, or parents. Or, they may simply have been persons in the congregation who encouraged us, who delighted in our growth and in "mothering" it. "Mothering" helps to give birth to the character the Holy Spirit wants to produce in us.

The ministry of encouragement does more than just draw out the growing character. It is one of the best ways of communicating good news. Words are important. Confrontation, communicating clearly are important. But the kind of spirit that draws forth is clearly and powerfully evangelistic. In a congregation, that ministry ought to prevail. Why? Because we belong first of all to the Paraclete. That ministry of comfort and encouragement, of interceding, of drawing forth, that is the ministry which Christ has given us. Ought not each of us live in such a way that the nickname Barnabas could be applied to us? Imagine! A whole church of Barnabases—sons and daughters of the encouraging Spirit of Jesus Christ. It would certainly help us be "of one heart and soul."

Discussion and Action

1. This study emphasizes the role of the ministry of encouragement. Is it that important? Find texts in Acts from your previous study or from other chapters in the New Testament to help you decide.
2. Can evangelism and encouragement be as closely related as they are in the lesson? How would "sons and daughters of the Paraclete" behave?
3. Share about the "Barnabases" who have helped you to grow in the faith.
4. Does a "ministry of encouragement" characterize your congregation? Your covenant group? Your own contributions in the congregation? Help each other find ways you can improve that situation.

10

"Who Me? A Leader?"
Acts 16:1-3, 11-15; Acts 18:24-28

Preparation

1. Study carefully the passages for this lesson. What qualifications did each of the persons mentioned in the scripture have to become a part of the ongoing story of the church?
2. Note some of the obscure names of the New Testament as you read. How are they drawn into the story in each case?

Understanding

Have you ever tried to count everyone mentioned in the book of Acts? They just keep coming. Person after person. Yet, in some special way, each helps carry on the story.

The Acts of the Apostles, we usually think, is a story about Peter and Paul. Really, it's a story of the Holy Spirit, a story of the way in which the Holy Spirit led the church in spreading the good news about Jesus, who is the Christ. And, while the focus seems to be on Peter and Paul, there are many, many others who join in the drama. We'll focus on a few of those others.

Each person has something to offer. In the Old Testament, for instance, Queen Esther found that because of her special position she would be able to help her people in a very difficult situation. But at the same time, she realized that doing so would put her in danger. So, she begged, "Can't someone else do it?" Mordecai answered that, yes, since it needs to be done, and you will not do it, our faithful God will likely raise up someone else to do it. But, he said, " . . . Who knows whether you have not come to the kingdom for such a time as this"

(Esth. 4:14). This was the one reason God needed Esther at that moment. A similar thing happens in Acts. Person after person finds the way in which God needs them at "such a time as this."

We want to look more closely at that discovery by four persons. The first is Timothy. Timothy was a special case. He needed to be "retrieved" just as Paul had been by Barnabas. Timothy was the son of a Jewish mother and a Greek father. And he had not been circumcised. That presented several difficulties to a Jew. First of all, to marry a Gentile was, for strict Jews, stepping outside the faith. Timothy's mother, therefore, though technically a Jew, was probably looked at somewhat askance by the Jewish community, especially since her son, who also was Jewish, had never been circumcised. It suggested that they showed little concern for their Jewish roots.

Paul recognized that if Timothy were to carry out a ministry in a primarily Jewish context, he should not bear what Jews would perceive as the stigma of disobedience. Jews would think it one thing for a Gentile not to have followed Jewish custom, but quite another for a Jew. Sensitive to all that, Paul had Timothy circumcised. In that act, Paul also showed that he could accept Timothy as a Jew, as well.

Timothy had an important place in the early church. He was a person upon whom others depended. Paul called him his "faithful child in the Lord." He sent Timothy as an emissary often because there was nobody who could understand Paul's mind quite so well or act and speak for Paul so well in nearly every situation. He could also be supportive of leadership, able to play second fiddle very well.

There were also the tentmakers Aquila and Priscilla, whom Paul probably met in Corinth. They may have been the persons who got Paul started in tentmaking and perhaps in ministry in Corinth. They had the ability, the capacity, to be the supportive, uplifting family that we so often need. They showed hospitality to Paul.

But there was something else about them, too. Apollos, about whom we want to speak more later, was a brilliant and powerful speaker, but he needed better understanding of the things he was talking about. Priscilla and Aquila took him aside. We suspect that Priscilla was the more able teacher of the two, recognizing accurate teaching, and helping those who perhaps had greater eloquence to do their work. So, in teaching, friendship, support, hospitality, Priscilla and Aquila responded to the call of the Holy Spirit.

Let's go back to Apollos. He was a Jew from Alexandria, the Harvard of Paul's day. An eloquent man, he knew the scriptures backwards and forwards. He had accurate information about Jesus, was evidently a disciple, and was apparently guided by the Holy Spirit. The text speaks of his being "fervent in spirit" and "bold" in speaking out. These are all gifts of the Spirit in Acts. But the scripture says he "knew only the baptism of John." That is usually associated with the strong call to repentance, the strong call to get your life in shape, live right, obey the ethical standards of the Law, do justice and mercy. Priscilla and Aquila missed in his preaching, however, the power to redeem and to renew. The baptism of Jesus is an empowering baptism which makes it possible through renewal and redirection of life to live what we are indeed called to do. The call to repentance alone can be depressing. Apollos was teachable, however. He learned from Priscilla and Aquila and became a powerful and bold voice.

One more: Lydia. Paul met Lydia in Philippi. In Philippi folks were very strict about Roman law. Foreign religions had to be practiced outside the city. Paul found Lydia and her group of women on the river bank in a "place of prayer." Among Lydia and her group, he found an openness he did not often find in the synagogue.

Lydia responded to the Holy Spirit with hospitality, first of all. "If you have judged me faithful," she said, "come and stay at my house." Lydia was head of a household and a seller of purple goods. She had to have some wealth for her business required much capital to maintain. But she was able to use her wealth with openness and exuberance for the good of the gospel and the spread of the church.

When Paul encourages those with the gift of generosity to use it in liberal giving, he must surely have been thinking of the example of Lydia and the Philippian church (Rom. 12:6-8). At Philippi there is no mention of Paul's working to make his own way as he did at Corinth. In marked contrast to the Corinthians, the church at Philippi gave freely, with no feeling that they were "buying" Paul's services.

These four, along with many others, were not the great lights of Acts, but they had an important part in carrying on the story. The story does not end with Acts. We, also, are expected to be ready to respond in the ways that the Lord makes possible for us.

Many people are just dripping with talent. We praise them and we think, "How wonderful they are." What do they amount to? Too often, they end up actually doing very little, other than creating status for themselves. And we hear little of it after they are gone. But a person whose talent has somehow been given back to the Lord and then received again may have a powerful and lasting impact.

Remember the story of the little fellow with the fishes and loaves (John 6:1-14)? When Jesus said, the people are hungry, the little fellow said, "I have some food." The trouble with adults is that when Jesus says, "The crowd is hungry," we don't respond because, after all, "All I have are a few fish and a bag of chips." The child thought what he had was enough, and he was able to place it in the hand of Jesus.

We need to be more like that little boy. When the Lord says the world is hungry, we need to be ready to say, "Well, I have a voice that trembles in public." The Lord will say, "It is enough." When the Lord says the world is confused, we need to be more ready to say, "I have a mind that can think through a few simple problems." Christ will say, "With my blessing, it is enough." "I have a house, a family, a fair reputation, a little impact in the community." "With my blessing, it is enough." That's the wonder. It *is* enough.

I once saw a sign referring to ministry. "The pay isn't much," it said, "but the benefits are out of this world." It's true. Be ready to answer the call. The important thing is not to maximize our talents, but to be ready to respond with all that we have and all that we are to the call of the Lord. Thus, the story begun in Acts can continue in our own time.

Discussion and Action

1. Spend time in your group, opening your bags of "fishes and loaves." What do you have in yours? Lay them out on the table. Then help each to see opportunities God is providing for the use of these "small" gifts for larger good.

2. Reflect together on the stories of Timothy, Priscilla and Aquila, Apollos, Lydia. Is there anything in their situations which touches yours? What? And how?

3. Discuss together ways that your group, your congregation can help the "lesser lights" in your fellowship to shine.